CRE8TVE SUCCESS

Inspire Your Customers, Amplify Your Profits
& Dominate Your Competition the
RIGHT (Brained) WAY

DAVID W LITWIN

PURE FUSION MEDIA
FRANKLIN, TENNESSEE

Pre-Release Sample Copy – This is a work in progress

All rights reserved. No part of this publication may be reproduced, stored in a retrieval system, or transmitted in any form or by any means—for example, electronic, photocopy, recording—without the prior permission of the publisher. The only exception is brief quotations in printed/online reviews.

Copyright © 2015 David Litwin
All rights reserved.
ISBN: 978-1518752698

INTRODUCTION

Do you know the **story** your customers share about your business? Have you crafted the *specific conversation* you want others to tell the world about your product or service?

More than any other time in history, story helps determine the success of a business. The meteoric rise of Internet sites like Yelp and Angie's List invigorated throngs of potential customers to open their computers, tablets, and smartphones and assess if a business' offerings are worth their hard-earned dollars. What metric do they often use to evaluate? Read some of the reviews on these sites. You'll be hard pressed to find itemized, point-by-point appraisals of a company's products or services. Instead, prepare to be inundated with *stories of the experience* they had with the company.

Did you catch that? Reviews on sites like Yelp or Angie's List rarely stop at the company's product or service. The reviews read like stories and the stories often focus on the experience. Successful companies don't merely produce great products and services; they know how to garner positive experiential stories. Without controlling your story and without focusing on the experience, you leave referrals to chance.

Stories do not just happen on desktops, laptops, and smartphones. Let me throw out a hypothetical scenario. Say you attend a cocktail party with friends. Prior to the party, you met with your current accountant and... well, things aren't working out. The relationship has soured, but it's tax time and you need someone to fill the gap quickly. During the evening, you share your frustration with a friend at the party. Let's suppose your friend offers two different referrals:

Referral 1: "I have an accountant, his name is John. He might be able to help..."

or

Referral 2:"You must call my accountant, John. He's got me so excited about my financial future!"

Which referral had more impact?

Did you notice the difference in tone, emphasis and action in the second referral? In the first referral, your friend explained he has an accountant named John, and that he might be of service. In the second referral, your friend could not wait to talk about John. One referral presented information. The other was peppered with emotion and personal assurance. One referral included facts; the other produced *inspiration*. When we are presented with facts, we process, evaluate, and often discard. When we are inspired, *we act*.

Let's talk about John from the second referral for a moment. The second John understood the power of the referral story, and specifically **designed** his business, and his business' experience, to produce those words and create that level of excitement and intensity. Your friend became John's ambassador. But the position wasn't left to chance. The "inspiring" story your friend told at that cocktail party was intricately interwoven into every aspect of John's business.

Your friend and the rest of John's clients spread powerful words about John's business. John knows *that* they tell his story. More importantly, he knows *what* story is told. How did he do it? To control his business' stories, John needed to think **creatively**. John, even though he's an accountant (and the furthest thing from, say, an artist), moved his business to the RIGHT and he has the success, clients and profits to prove it.

You might be asking yourself, what does it mean to move my business to the right? Am I supposed to switch political parties? Should I stick Rush Limbaugh on my call waiting soundtrack? The right I am referring to isn't political; it's neurological. Success and influence have shifted to those able to capitalize on right brain *thinking*.

WHAT *IS* RIGHT (BRAINED) THINKING?

While we are each unique, we think in similar patterns. Whenever we think or act, we operate out of two regions, or two brain hemispheres, the Left or the Right. For the sake of brevity, I will quickly break down the difference in thought and action between the left and right brained:

If you are left brained, you are most likely influenced by numbers, facts, routine, order, and logic. Vocationally, you might be an accountant, a math or science teacher, an I.T.

specialist, a draftsman, an insurance salesperson, or the owner of one of these types of businesses.

If you are right brained, you are more likely ruled by creativity, metaphor, visual beauty, and lyric. Vocationally, you might be a graphic designer, a musician, an author or singer, a painter, or even a salesperson.

There are numerous books spotlighting the differences in left and right brain thinking for psychological and interpersonal motivations. This book harnesses the principles, or "operating energies," of a right brain thinker for the sake of *business* success. We will peer into the psyche and history of right brain thinkers, extracting what makes them instrumental in our lives today. We will then apply those findings to the shaping and crafting our businesses, companies, non-profits, sales processes, and the like for greater customer loyalty and increased profitability.

For the past forty-plus years, technology, media, publishing, and education have evolved from left to right brain thought.

What about business?

Granted, there are more creative agencies and companies run by right brain thinkers in the U.S. today than at any other time in history. But what about your business? In today's world of automation and commoditization, a right brain business approach is essential. When the economy goes down and your service or product prices tumble, you must stand out. When the economic tide rises, you must avoid losing business and market share to those that can automate your skillsets and/or products into binary code and make you and your business irrelevant.

This book teaches you to craft and design your business and your business experience. Craft and design are very right brain words. Allow me to give you a few more: create, story tell, shape, and compose. By using the energies of the artist, the poet, the scriptwriter, the musician, and the designer you can create a business producing more loyal customers and the strongest of referrals.

Though the storyteller, poet, musician, artist, and designer are not always the highest paid members of our society (everyone in Los Angeles has a script, and everyone in Nashville has a song catalog), they change *how* you view the world. They are world creators, perception skewers. You will use their energies to create the perception you want to share of your world of accounting, pharmaceutical sales, insurance, architecture, or any other vocational field.

Because, if Daniel Pink, New York Times and Wall Street Journal best selling author, is right (and I believe he is), this is now a right brain world, baby! You must adapt or perish, recreate or be crushed. It happens every day. Failed businesses put "For Lease" signs on their now empty office spaces after solely relying on the left brain idea that they only need their product or service to generate revenue. It worked for around the last 150 years, but it isn't going to work as well now. In *Knowledge Worker,* Peter Drucker posited that left brain thinkers would flourish in the modern economy. For a time, his predictions held true. But that era is nearly over. Now, it's, "long live the creatives," or, better yet, the creative *thinkers.*

It's a radical shift, but it is not as hard a shift as it used to be. The technologies, ideologies, and worldviews of today allowed it to occur. A creative thirteen year old YouTube sensation now gets a million dollar endorsement contract in the blink of an eye. That might take over 10,000 customers through your hairstyling business or 500+ customers through your tax accounting firm. It took a year of blood, sweat, and tears for you to make that kind of money. It took the kid a few hours (at least to sign the contract). The rise of information transmission and the embrace of form over function have broken rigidity, the status quo, the logical, and the literal.

Do not think this means creative companies, those providing right-brain *products or services*, are given a pass. You can own a graphic design company but still think with the left brain when it comes to the design *of your business and business experience*, not your art. Highly creative individuals fail to get their companies out of the basement, because they forget to apply the very context of what they do to their own small business practices. I take market share away from these individuals every day.

In this book, I will discuss the what's, why's, and how's of this right brain shift. Then we will look at designing a business and creating the story that you want to tell and you want your clients to tell about your offerings. Finally, we will look at what to do when you achieve success.

STRIVING FOR SIGNIFICANCE

I believe that if you follow the steps and principles in this book, you will not only gain financial success, *you will also strive for significance*. You will create meaning for yourself, your customers, your business, and the world. Rather than pushing widgets or strictly selling services you will inspire others to live with passion, interest, and drive.

I've written three books. Four, if you count a 50-page ebook. I did not mean to write books. I tried writing simple blog posts. Then blog posts turned into articles, which grew into ebooks, which became *the length* of books, so I published them. In writing these books, I attempted to teach people to see value in their world, in themselves, and, since I've written on theology, in their faith.

If I am going to write another book, it is not just going to be about making money. I believe everyone on this planet is inherently capable of making a difference in this world. Many people never realize it. They let 'Resistance' (the personification of fear and procrastination) win as spotlighted in the *War of Art* by Stephen Pressfield (I highly recommend reading his book).

That's tragic.

Even more tragic are the ones that *do* make it: those that have the *capacity* to produce significance and meaning, but focus success back onto themselves. They often become, like Scorcese's *Wolf of Wall Street*, shallow, husks of men and women that had it all, only to become caricatures for others' amusement. It is not funny to those in their relational circles.

Instead, the world needs more Bono's.

It needs more men and women that do not just accumulate stuff, but use their stuff *to make a difference.* Maybe you are next. Before you dust off the Stratacaster, I think you can get there through your business. It does not matter whether you provide left brain or right brain services, whether you're a financial analyst or a studio musician, these principles and action items allow you to rise to the top of your profession and tower over your competition while providing benefits to humanity.

    I am excited. I hope you are. The journey begins for both of us now. You see, I wrote this chapter prior to writing the book. I hope I gain as much insight in the writing of this book as I believe you will gain in reading it.

    Live Inspired.

HOW TO READ THIS BOOK

Each chapter of this book is broken into two sections, both with identical content; based on the right or left brained temperament of the reader. The first section of each chapter contains visuals and text content that play off the creative tendencies of those with *right brain* proclivities. The second section is written in the standard line-by-line format of most writings; which plays more into the temperament of a *left brain* thinker.

You can choose to focus on the first section of each chapter and easily read the entire book in less than 20 minutes. For some, in an age where time is both precious and fleeting, this may be enough. For others, the first section will serve as an overview of the chapter, which can be delved into in more detail after reading the second section of the chapter. If you are completely left brained, you might avoid those "pesky" visuals altogether and strictly read the second section of each chapter.

Regardless of how you choose to engage this book, I encourage you to read the "Action Items" section at the end of most chapters. These are practical questions and recommendations that allow you to apply the teachings presented in this book for even more business success, significance, and influence.

If you have any thoughts, comments, or insights while reading, or would like to schedule a *design, story, and meaning consultation* for your business, feel free to reach out to me at: david@purefusionmedia.com - I love thoughtful, interactive dialog, so don't be afraid to engage.

CHAPTER 1 | # "THINKING" ON THE RIGHT SIDE OF THE BRAIN

Left and Right Brain thinkers see the world (and our hands) very differently:

LEFT BRAIN DRAWING

RIGHT BRAIN DRAWING

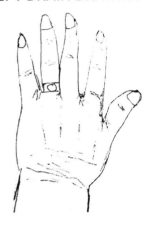

The Left Brain focuses on the appearance of a hand, considering the fingers and nails as items. Left brain doesn't focus on shape, tone or texture.

The Right Brain doesn't look at the "hand," but the shapes, curves and lines that form the hand. It creates a realistic intrepetation of shape and form.

DIFFERENCES BETWEEN THE LEFT AND RIGHT BRAIN

(LAST 150 YEARS)
LEFT BRAIN:
Analysis
Sequencing (Deconstructive)
Reason
Literal
Logic
Compartmentalism
Science (of the past)

"Knowledge Workers"
(PETER DRUCKER)

(LAST 30-40 YEARS)
RIGHT BRAIN:
Insight
Connectedness
Creativity
Metaphorical
Discernment
Meaning
Spirituality

"World Creators"

Left Brain thinkers like order, they like reason; facts and figures, numbers and graphs.

Right Brain thinkers like creativity, aesthetics, meaning, painting, metaphor, beauty

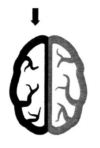

LEFT BRAIN: Asks "What" and "How"

RIGHT BRAIN: Asks "Why"

RIGHT BRAIN (World Creators):

Shape and craft how we view the world through art, story, lyric and note.

LEFT BRAIN COMPANIES:

AUTOMATED (times of abundance)   **COMMODITIES** (times of lack)   **IRRELEVANT** (always)

{ A **Right Brain Thinking Company** uses the traits of a Right Brain Thinker to create an "Experience" that transcends automation, commodization and irrelevancy. }

CHAPTER 1

"THINKING" ON THE RIGHT SIDE OF THE BRAIN

I founded two highly successful design agencies and have been a graphic designer for nearly three decades. My firms have provided creative services for some of the most well known Fortune 500 companies in the world. I started my current company, Pure Fusion Media, with under a thousand dollars, and because of my creative skillsets and strategic business dealings, I cleared 25K the first month and over three million in the first two years. Visual design has dominated my life and filled my coffers since the late 1980s. But before I turned seventeen, I was anything but an artist.

    I remember my first high school art class. The initial assignment was to draw your hand. I did my best; drawing something Picasso would have gagged at. Somewhat sheepishly, I handed my poor attempt to the teacher. "Well, that is certainly a *left brain* rendition of a hand," she chuckled.

I did not know what that meant. Back then, none of us did.

The next day, she had us draw our hands again. Instead of the safety of looking at the paper, we had to draw "what we saw" – without looking down. You can imagine how hard is to shape forms without assessing your progress. Once finished, I looked down at the paper. I was surprised how much better the hand looked than the "left brain rendition" of the hand I had drawn the previous day. Sure, fingernails failed to line up with fingers, and lines went up into nowhere, but I could tell it had the inklings of a somewhat realistic looking hand.

The following day, the new assignment was to *combine* the two techniques. We were allowed to look at the paper, but only to center our lines or to make sure that fingernails lined up, etc. I crafted shapes and tones, looking down only when necessary as the teacher requested. After completion, I surveyed the whole of my drawing.

I had drawn a hand!

Not the idea of a hand, but a lifelike hand, one that appeared to be coming out of the paper into three-dimensional space. I could not believe it! I showed it to the teacher. She could not believe it either. "Class," she said, "this young man is shifting his brain from left to right."

That night, I went home and drew hands. I drew lots of hands. Hands open, hands clenched. Palm up, palm down, any way I could draw a hand. This time, I took the paper to school and proudly handed it to the teacher. At parent/teacher night that next week, I was the visual example of her experiment in teaching from a revolutionary new book entitled, *Drawing on the Right Side of the Brain* by Betty Edwards.

Today, we pretty much understand left and right brain dynamics. Back then, only a few years after the invention of the fRMI machine, this was a revolutionary concept. I am a success story of that teaching and its transforming power in my life. It changed the course of my future.

Don't pick up a drawing pencil just yet (although you might want to get Edwards' book). **The point is, right brain and left brain centric people see the world (or, in the case of my art class: our hands) very differently.**

THINKING WITH THE RIGHT SIDE OF YOUR BRAIN

What does it look like to *think* with the right side of the brain? Let us reflect on the difference in thought between the left and right brain thinker.

LEFT BRAIN THINKING	**RIGHT BRAIN THINKING**
Analysis	Insight
Sequencing (deconstructive)	Synergy
Reason	Creativity
Literal	Metaphorical
Logic	Discernment
Compartmentalism	Meaning
Fueled on the sciences of the past	Spirituality (of the past and present)
"Knowledge Workers"	**"World Creators"**

Left brain thinkers like order, reason, facts, figures, numbers, and graphs. Give them the facts and let them run with them. No debate needed, no additional thought required. They rarely connect many dots, unless the facts require it, and they are very literal. One plus One equals two, it does not equal four, and it certainly does not equal color, tone or lyric. Science is broken into different and separate parts, known as "reductionism:" "Let us learn all we can about X and then we will learn all we can about Y." But X *in relation* to Y is seldom considered.

Left brain thinkers often excel (at least in the past) in school. They are especially proficient in math, science and logic. If you aced your Trig and Chem classes, but struggled in Creative Writing 101, you might be left brained.

Right brain thinkers are harder to pin down. To a left brain thinker, they are nuts. Where analysis dominates the left brained thinker, the right brain thinker wants more insight. The left brain thinker focuses on what and how; the right brain thinker asks, "why?" Right-brained people often refuse to be told the correct or reasoned way to do something. They want to blaze their own trail, even if the answer fails to make logical sense. Left brain thinkers focus on facts; right brain thinkers like stories and the more creative the story the better.

Right brain thinkers fixate on the aesthetic and its many forms. They love and create novels and screenplays, songs, poetry, paintings, pottery, and the like. They are often fashion designers, creative app developers, product designers, or movie directors. Left brain thinkers play Words with Friends against the computer. Right Brain thinkers spend hours playing The Sims in massively multiplayer environments.

KNOWLEDGE WORKERS vs. WORLD CREATORS

Peter Drucker described those that excel at left brain thought as "Knowledge Workers." I will describe right brain thinkers as "World Creators." **World Creators craft new and innovative ways of seeing the world – and ourselves.** Remember *The Matrix*? The movie not only created a digital world, it left you with a new way of looking at *the real world*. How many times has your life been affected by a song or a book? For many country music listeners, the song "I Hope You Dance" changed their view on the value of life. For most of the rest of us, pick about any song by the Beatles.

Think about the teachers that inspired you. What caused the inspiration? Was it that they spoke about the particulars of geometry in rote formulas, or did they connect geometry to life so that it resonated deep inside your soul? I once read a highly secular, highly anti-religious book encouraging history professors to present the subject as little more than dates and names (or, as my good friend Stephen Mansfield penned, little more than "Dates and Dead People.") According to the book, if a student equated meaning to history he or she might question naturalism and the random-chance nature of the secularized, religious-free life.

Forget that!

My favorite teacher during my education was a college history teacher that "showed" us history and its connectedness. He didn't teach history in "fill in the blank" fashion.

What about business? Or, better yet...

WHY BUILD A RIGHT BRAIN THINKING COMPANY?

Here is the bomb drop.

Left brain thinking companies often become irrelevant, commodities, or automated.

I took typing in junior high school. I got up to about 50 words per minute. I took typing... using a typewriter. Ask anyone under twenty what a typewriter is, and you are likely to get blank stares. The typewriter produced some of the finest creations from both the right and left brained alike for well over a century and, a few stalwart authors aside, it is gone. The function of the typewriter was replaced by an entirely new functioning invention that swallowed up the product.

Before traveling to Hawaii in the early nineties I bought about five disposable cameras to mark my trip (well, mostly to take pictures of the women we met, but I digress). Back then, they were on the impulse shelves at the front of every grocery store. Seen any recently?

Even new inventive products like FitBit, putting millions into their "cool," right brain focused hardware and software, risk being gobbled up by a single app on the Apple Watch. As long as someone can build something that assimilates our product or service into itself, we are in jeopardy - if we *only* focus on our product or service.

How about *commoditization* and *automation*?

They are often directly correlated America's fiscal status. In times of great growth, people a lot smarter than us build products that *automate* what we bank our futures on. In times of lack, people with less skill than us use those newly invented products to undercut the market, and our industry suffers from *commoditization*. During the growth of automation, the speed of the product goes up and the price of the product goes down, making entry into your market easier and easier. During the growth of commoditization, the number of individuals in your market goes up, and *your* pricing goes down. In our "flattened" world, you are competing with people from China, India and Pakistan willing to work for ten times less than you or your workers and still live like kings.

How can you compete with that?

I have survived through three shifts in this automation/commoditization quagmire. The first was the ***desktop publishing*** onslaught, where everyone who bought the programs Pagemaker or Quark Express thought they were graphic designers. I often fought for business against the 18 year old with no experience or the 65 year old scrapbook mom who pursued design after the friends in her coffee klatch told her how good her scrapbook boards were.

Five or so years later, the ***web designer*** wave exploded onto the creative marketplace. Now everyone who bought FrontPage, Dreamweaver or Flash thought they could become web design gurus. The market again flooded with fresh new "creatives," producing websites with no structure, no forethought and no marketing strategy. Still, most prices were economical, so people paid 1/5 of the amount I charged at my firm to be, "up on the web." Two to four years later, I snatched up all those companies' website redesigns.

We are now in an even more complex shift. Employing new strategies are essential for survival. Enter the era of ***crowdsourcing***. Crowdsourcing is a small agency killer. Crowdsourcing sites make millions on creatives who either "bid" on *potential* projects or "compete" for a client's business – with the rest of the *global* community. What used to be a flooded market that would undercut your agency for 1/5th the price is now bid out to designers who will do the work for free, in hopes of getting a project for 1/10th of the standard small agency price.

Bigger and bigger companies are realizing the value of crowdsourcing, taking business away from the design conglomerates and handing it to the best of the best single shop creatives in Romania, Russia, Brazil, Pakistan, etc. Why not? You can now avoid the big agency's overhead and get better design for 1/10th to 1/100th of the price, depending on the agency you *used* to work with.

I can't compete with Romania or Pakistan – if it all were focused on price. So price is not my focus. I've applied the principles in this book and centered my attention on *the experience*. I crafted my ethics, as you will soon discover, to ensure success beyond my services, and I created a powerful story that gets discussed often. But that is getting ahead of ourselves a bit.

SURVIVING AND THRIVING

Let me tell you how I not only survived, but also thrived, during this crowdsourcing wave. I started in the early 2000s with decent sized agency of ten creatives. But I never saw my family. I was always at work, stressed over keeping my internal employees happy while juggling a large book of business. A few years later, I read Timothy Ferriss' book, *4 Hour Work Week*. Around halfway through the book, I embraced the idea of outsourcing and streamlining my business practices. I shifted my entire business model to outsourcing projects to local and national designers and keeping the company sleek and fluid.

When the crowdsourcing model exploded, I noticed prices dropping and many expressing frustration over losing to single shop designers across the globe. I refused to add my voice to the dissention. Instead, I scoured these sites for the best of the best creatives. Finding their websites or email addresses, I sent direct messages, offering them the opportunity for *guaranteed* work rather than the erratic speculation of the global creative market.

"I hired skilled and affordable contractors from around the globe, paid them a competitive wage, and gave them the stability that they sought, while allowing me more time to cultivate and grow the creative aspects of my business." This also allows me the opportunity to engage in other activities, including the writing of this book.

The tides are changing. The waves of irrelevance, commoditization and automation swell ever higher. Today, you cannot simply survive the wave. You need to ride it. Then you must create new waves and let the power of all this right brain inventiveness broadcast its effects out into the world.

To understand the tide changes we must understand where we have been, and where we find ourselves today. The next chapter is a bit of a history lesson. It serves as a powerful understanding of *why* we went right, and how to see your path to navigate.

CHAPTER 2 | # HOW BUSINESS MOVED RIGHT

America has been predominantly a LEFT BRAIN thinking culture for centuries.

(BIGGER MACHINES)  (MORE WORKERS)

THE INDUSTRIAL REVOLUTION

Invention was mostly about FUNCTION, not form.

It was the WEALTHY that could afford the aesthetic, form-based offerings of the right brained.

ART   JEWELRY   SCULPTURE

But what about the REST OF SOCIETY?

 EDUCATE BASED ON KNOWLEDGE
{ Math and Sciences }

 Brightest in LEFT BRAIN attributes rose to the top and transcended the worker class.

WORLD WARS I and II

Tanks, Guns, Planes didn't have to look good, they had to function perfectly.

ALLIES WIN!
National Pride
Business Growth
Traditional Values

THEN CAME THE 60s

Counter Cultural
Rebelious
Searching for Meaning

These are disciplines of the RIGHT BRAIN

REBELLION NEEDED A VOICE

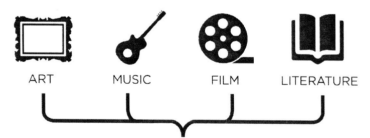

ART   MUSIC   FILM   LITERATURE

RIGHT BRAIN developments

ATTITUDES OF THE 1960S SHIFTED THE BUSINESS WORLD

Brightest in RIGHT BRAIN attributes began to be recruited by businesses.

People fought for Individualism

INDIVIDUALITY ➡ NEW INVENTION

| Style requires Creativity | THE EMBRACE OF *Style* | Things were judged on how they looked not how they functioned |

THE PERSONAL COMPUTER (MACINTOSH)

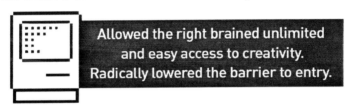

Allowed the right brained unlimited and easy access to creativity. Radically lowered the barrier to entry.

INCREASED CREATIVITY = THE NEED TO SHARE!

ENTER **THE INTERNET**

Class, age and education barriers shattered. No valid metrics.

Success became based on (Global) Subjectivity

Now - RIGHT BRAINED CEOs hire the brightest Left Brain Thinkers to staff IT or run the accounting department.

LESSON LEARNED?

If society has shifted from Left Brain to Right Brain, then businesses need to make THE CUSTOMER EXPERIENCE more valuable than money.

CHAPTER 2:

HOW BUSINESS MOVED RIGHT

For at least the last 150 years, left brain centric thought dominated and accelerated American society. But the left brain shift incubated earlier in America's history. Fueled on the scientific discoveries and philosophical ideologies of the previous 100 years, the **industrial revolution** exploded into the U.S. landscape in the late 1700s. It brought a rise to inventiveness like the world had seldom seen. Unlike the inventions of the previous millennia, the production machines that crafted and assembled these inventions were so gargantuan they required myriad of individuals to see them realized. Factories were filled to the brim with workers. Salesmen flooded the suburban and city streets peddling new ideas.
    But invention *was predominately about function*.

We were learning new and better ways of *accomplishing* things. Neil Postman in his book, *Technopoly,* describes our cultural shift from a tool-based society (slow and limited) to a technocracy (automated tools and technologies allow us to function efficiently) to a Technopoly (technology now dominates us... and that's bad). The hand led to the hammer, which led to the nail gun, which lead the automated machine, which led to the hand becoming irrelevant. Musician Jack Johnson stated.

"Our feet became the wheels
and the wheels became the cars
and then the rigs began to drill
until the drilling goes too far."

That is a singer songwriter crafting an ecological point lyrically, but you get the idea. We spent nearly two hundred years in United States crafting more efficient ways of *functioning*. Invention was based on utility. Price was often dictated on the performance of that utility. You didn't pay more for a typewriter in the 1940s by how it looked, but according to what additional functions it accomplished. Aesthetic design was employed on right brain activities, such as the look and feel of a violin or the crafting of fine china bowls.

(DON'T) BLAME IT ON THE RICH!

The rich could afford to own something *beyond* utility. They had often made their money off the backs of those having fabricated their left-brain utilitarian inventions in their factories. While the rich could appreciate creations crafted by right brain thinkers, such as expensive paintings, fine architecture and the opulence of high priced jewelry and sculpture, the rest of the society was often *forced* to think left.

Since the rich only constitute about 1% of the population as the Occupy Wall Street folks mused, thought needed to shift toward educating the other 99%. If the focus were utility and expanding the reach of utility, then the training of the young would be based on knowledge. Invention is often birthed out of the fetal tissue of science and math, so train the youth in rigid principles, that, when combined, produced inventiveness and societal usefulness.

Those lucky few that rose to the Knowledge-based surface experienced the luxury of transcending the life of the menial worker. Thinking with the full capacity of the left brain often allowed these individuals to accelerate the ranks, collect wealth, and then also invest in the aesthetic creations designed by those on the right.

If design was only afforded to the rich or the esoteric, let the eccentrics of the world focus on their needs. At the ground level, we need left brain geniuses to invent cars, planes, boats, road paving machines, etc. We need the rest of the populace to construct and assemble those inventions. Left brain education filtered out the executives, the managers, and the menial workers.

The rise of left brain thought, both culturally and academically, was not bad or erroneous. It was necessary for societal growth. America was a baby eagle stretching its legs. Those legs didn't need to be fashioned with Ugg boots quite yet.

Two **World Wars** stoked the flames of left brain innovation. In the cross hairs of your enemy you didn't need a gun, tank or plane to look good. You wanted that invention to work, and work as efficiently as possible. Factories created disparate, uninspiring parts that were finally put together in another factory to form a plane, tank or gun. So the right brained in the ranks painted pretty ladies on the side of their B52's fuselauge to give the gray or camoflauge some life and character. Then tragically across Europe, Africa and Asia, bombs and bullets destroyed millennia of right brain art and architecture.

The horror of Pearl Harbor aside, war never reached the continental United States. While the rest of the world was digging out and rebuilding after the Second World War, the United States boomed, technologically and fiscally.

But a new shift was on the tide...

Tom Brokaw heralded the World War II Generation as the "Greatest Generation." The Industrial Revolution often led to greed, class warfare and distaste of the fellow man beneath you. War brought the country together as one. We had won, and we did it together. Yet in all the power, value and performance inventiveness of left brain thinking, it began to wane.

People wanted more. They were no longer content with the logical and literal. But the clarion call didn't come from society's leaders. It came from those many would call society's deviants.

IT'S ALL ABOUT ORIGINALITY, MAN...

While the Left-Brain rich rested in their ivory towers convinced the world would never change, many of those never making the grade to Knowledge Worker started congregating.

Their dissention was more ideological than neurological. They weren't rebelling against the left brain. The protested *the ideals* of the left brain: order, control, unabated commitment, and reason. They questioned the path to success of the Knowledge Worker and their wealthy employers. To the rebel, there was no meaning in it. No heart.

Questioning the status quo, logic and reason is, by its very nature, a shift toward the right. This dissention needed a voice, a transmission mechanism. Since these rebels were already thinking toward the right, why not use the tools of the right to broadcast the message? The voice of left brain dissention did not come out of America's mechanics or its government, but through paint, lyric and note. Americans artistically viewed and lyrically listened to a new way of thinking. It wasn't about fiscal and technological progress. It was about meaning and purpose and embracing of the great questions of life.

It was also laced with drugs, protest and violence, but the intention was to celebrate individuality and rebel against conformity and dogma. Rebellion is often considered erroneous by the party in charge. I remember a line from the brilliant film, *The Count of Monte Cristo*: *"In the end, treason is just a matter of dates."* I don't subscribe to that idiom, but it brings up a valid point. When Orwell penned *1984*, it was a literary celebration of the right brain mind, followed quickly by oppression and subjugation from the left brain mind.

The embrace of individuality led to new invention. Not of utility, *but of style*. People wanted to celebrate their uniqueness, so companies needed to create products embracing *individuality*. This is not a left brain virtue. Order and conformity fill the edifices of the left brained. It did not require

Knowledge to design with style and individuality. It required *creativity*. By the time the beat poets, authors and artists reached their early thirties, the really smart and innovative left brained thinkers started employing them.

The auto conglomerate sat in his office scheming: "I've got all the left brain Knowledge Workers making the highest *performance* vehicle possible, now I need the right brain artists to make it *look good*." The elite snatched up right brain individuals from obscurity and poverty. Quickly, these new right brain workers surpassed the financial status of their left brained coworkers, yet rarely reached the success pinnacle of their employer.

THE AUTOMATION EXPLOSION

Then this budding right brain thinking collided with the digital age. The original Turing machines and the IBM computer were created to serve specific purposes. But the ***personal* computer** was developed to serve a person's uniqueness.

In the early world of DOS, creativity was led by the most creative left brained thinkers. You couldn't *see* what you were designing. Coding looked a lot like math and science. But as we reached Orwell's year of supposed domination, 1984, Apple and IBM released the first versions of the WYSIWIG (what you see is what you get) operating system. The Window's version predominantly thought left, so the creative world embraced one of the first right brain technological edifices, the **Macintosh**. Inside the camel colored box was a utopia of left brained thinking and components. On the screen, it was a right brain fantasy world.

High school computer classes shifted from analytics and calculation to digital art. The left brained rich were losing their grip, but with enough right brain workers in their arsenal, they could retain a bit of market share.

As a general rule, people don't want to create in obscurity. They want to share, to interact. Woodstock was more than a music gathering; it evidenced the individual's desire to connect in their individuality. And so **the internet** was created. Through the web, *everything* changed.

Not only could we communicate with each other globally, we could also create things that *were better* than others. Then the global audience could evaluate what was beneficial and what should be discarded. The world was not only flat – class structure was obliterated. It didn't matter if you were a corporate mogul with three Phd's or a twenty year old high school dropout. If the public spoke, the dropout was in and the mogul was out. Creativity now rules the day. The final nail in the function-centric coffin of the Left-Brain elite had been pounded down… hard.

Left brain thought contained logical, quantifiable success parameters. With the Internet, success needed no metric. Fame and fortune became a *subjective phenomenon*. And subjectivity is a byproduct of the right brain.

Culturally, it is no longer the Left Brained at the corporate business head, surrounded by a cadre of Knowledge workers and a few right brained workers to beautify the product or visually market the service. **It is now Right Brained executives**, hiring other right brained workers, and employing a few left brained workers to create the web or app code, run the I.T. department and staff accounting. Sales moved from the regurgitation of figures and statistics, to creative thinking and story generation. Human resource departments now invent innovative and creative ways of keeping their employees satisfied, from Yoga classes to the recommendation of holistic medicine, certainly disciplines of the right.

The Internet allowed for the meteoric rise of... anyone. Anyone with a video camera, typing or design skills can experience success, fame, and fortune today. It doesn't even have to be human. Grumpy Cat made tens of millions of dollars for simply being... a grumpy cat. What's utilitarian about that? Attractive girls like the two sweethearts of *#EleventhGorgeous* garner huge contracts by staid beauty conglomerations for simply putting on makeup and being kitschy and cute. Billion dollar companies now take advice from creative 14 year olds with 2 million subscribers on YouTube.

NOW ABOUT YOU

You've got to compete in all of that. You must create a way to get noticed by the regional, national or global audience. Sure, you need to use social media to get your product or service out in the market, but so is your competition. You need to differentiate yourself from *everybody* out there.

How are you going to do it? Naturally, to be successful, you need to make your customer's time, and your products and/or services more valuable then their money. Your customers have to believe in the value of your offerings over their hard earned finances.

But this chapter has taught us is that success has shifted beyond those initial parameters.

The new standard is that you also have to make *the experience* of working with you and your business more valuable than their money. And for that, you need to think like the right brained. You need to employ design. You need to master storytelling. You need to weave intentional creativity into every aspect of the customer experience.

For the right brained, this chapter may read like a cumbersome history lesson (although I did my best to respect your temperament). Regardless, there was a crucial point to this exercise. By understanding the societal shift toward right brain thinking and design, you can see what and how your customers are thinking and how they now engage. Hopefully, you've also recognized the need to employ right brain thought and design into *your* business.

No, I do not just mean hire a great graphic designer or agency to market and message your operation, though you will soon see that is essential. You must design the *processes and standards* of your business. You are about to learn how to become an artist, composer and storyteller of *everything* about your company – not just your products or services – through design, story and meaning. I will start with a new way of looking at *design*.

A QUICK CAVEAT: WHEN TOO MUCH RIGHT GOES WRONG

Upon finishing this chapter, I forwarded it to a number of my closest friends. Receiving positive feedback, I pressed forward with minor grammar edits - until I got a call. It was from a good friend of mine who works with government contracts in the defense industry. Most people were inspired, even liberated by this chapter. He was downtrodden. He had seen a blitzkrieg of right brain marketing hype and emotional decisions influence contracts at the highest and most crucial of levels. In his industry, pragmatics and professional standards had eroded, leaving those defending our nation with products and equipment that he considered subpar and counter intuitive. The dangerous implications of all right brained society were very real to him.

I do not believe in a right brained domineering utopia, as was his fear. Too much right brained acceptance, too much emotional decision making, and quality and professional standards are replaced by well crafted marketing hype. Manufactured obsolescence and poor craftsmanship can be justified through the right "brand messaging." Left brain dominance may have eroded culturally, but its positive characteristics of decency, structural significance, quality, and respect must never be forgotten. In *1984*, Orwell proposed that a Left Brain domineering society would imprison us. Neil Postman in *Amusing Ourselves to Death*, posited that we were dangerously becoming more like the right brain domineering culture of Huxley's, *A Brave New World*. Neither Orwell's or Huxley's conceptualizations should have any place in a prosperous, creative and empathetic society.

CHAPTER 3 | **(BUSINESS) DESIGN**

DESIGN

DANIEL PINK — "To take what already exists and transform it into something new..." (A Whole New Mind)

DAVID W LITWIN — "... and hopefully **revelatory!**"

"FOR EVERY 1 PERCENT OF SALES INVESTED IN PRODUCT DESIGN, A COMPANY'S SALES AND PROFITS RISE BY AN AVERAGE OF 3 TO 4 PERCENT."
(Daniel Pink, A Whole New Mind)

Standard thinking is that Business Design
means ARTWORK

BUT DESIGN IS:

- Creative
- Unique
- Significant
- Intentional

} Why not apply these "design" traits to your **BUSINESS EXPERIENCE**

Design a creative and unique experience for your customer and you set yourself apart in the marketplace.

THIS REQUIRES INTENTIONALITY!

CHAPTER 3:

(BUSINESS) DESIGN

"There is nothing new under the sun…"

… Said the famous poet, philosopher and king – Solomon. The same mantra applies to most design. For the painter, the paint already exists. For the musician, the notes are already available. For the poet or scriptwriter, the words have already been created. How the paint, notes and words *are combined* determines the value and wonder of the art, composition or poetry.

Daniel Pink, in his book *A Whole New Mind*, describes design as *"to take what already exists and transform it into something new…"* and, I would add: "… and hopefully *revelatory*." Design requires us to understand the components of our craft, only to learn new and innovative ways of orchestrating those components to produce something radical and disruptive.

Integrating design is essential for any successful company. Pink explains that, according to the London Business School, *"For every percent of sales invested in product design, a company's sales and profits rise by an average of 3 to 4 percent."* That number is fairly significant. I can go considerably higher.

During the height of the recession, my current agency rebranded a Nashville-based limousine operation. The initial request called for an updated website. After scrutinizing their original branding and messaging, we assured the client that a brand overhaul was needed. Applying a poor brand over a fresh and relevant web design was not going to produce success, nor synergize with *our ethics*, a concept you will discover shortly.

Skeptical at first, the company agreed to our recommendation. In the information-gathering interview, using our Needs Based Analysis Questionnaire (NBA), we asked them to outline the project's Conditions of Satisfaction. Among those conditions was the criterion that the new branding and site increase revenue by 25% over the next year.

We nearly *doubled* their revenue in six months.

During the height of a recession a luxury service experienced unfettered growth. When other businesses were battening down the financial hatches, this newly branded, high dollar operation was bursting at the seams. You will view that brand later in this book.

Three years before the downturn in the economy, we rebranded a non-profit, the oldest day home for inner city children in the country. They were skeptical and cautious at first. After all, they were a non-profit. But we assured them of the value of the image shift. They *tripled* the amount procured from corporate donations that year.

The new image evoked something powerful in the day home's ambassadors. They were so excited about the new imagery that it translated into positive energy on their faces and smiles. When corporate donors observed that energy, they felt inclined to invest more money.

People often argue with me, especially in the South. They question, "Why should I pay your agency rates when I know a guy who knows a designer that can design my logo for $50 bucks?" Decent design looks attractive. Good design may produce compliments. But **exceptional design generates power, effective action, and trust.**

I'm getting ahead of myself a bit. I have presented business design through the standard lens: that of artwork. This is often where our perception of business design ends. That is tragic. It is also unprofitable. Consider the nature of design for a few moments. Design is more than visual artistic beauty. Starting with the obvious…

Design is Creative

Great design, no matter the medium, requires creativity. We must step outside of the box and look at things from a new angle, a fresh perspective. With a few exceptions, the more creative the design, the most interest it garners. Creativity evokes action. Consider for example, that scriptwriting generally followed a standard, three-act format for decades. Then Quentin Tarantino turned scriptwriting on its head with films like *Pulp Fiction*. His film, and its format, shifted the status quo. It created a new style other scriptwriters soon embodied.

Design is Unique

We separate one design from another by its uniqueness. Songwriters and music artists spend countless dollars in litigations after the notes of a new song resemble the musical structure of a previous musical track. When we look at Picasso, we do not see Monet's work. While design is often influenced by past work, it must retain it's own unique characteristics or it is not design, it is plagiarism.

Like *Pulp Fiction*, or Elvis, or the Beatles, when something really unique comes along, we celebrate it with fervor. If we design something that has not previously hit the societal landscape, we often experience years, decades, or centuries of success. Now, with the Internet, unique design can populate and propagate in nanoseconds.

Design is Significant

As I stated before, design should be revelatory. It should evoke a visceral response leading to a change in perception. Think about the great art, music, lyric or literature experienced in your life. Has it changed your perception of the world? Has a form of design shifted the entire course of your vocational future? Think about how many people became painters and photographers after viewing the works of Warhol; musicians after listening to The Beatles; authors after reading Hemingway. Design, not just historically, but also holistically, produces significance.

Design is Intentional

Design is purposeful; it has intent. Even if that intent is to make money, there is something driving the artist, the musician, the poet, and the scriptwriter. For most of the right brained, it is more about the experience than the final result. Whether for selfish or altruistic reasons, there is intent behind design.

Design is also intentional in that it takes work, focus, and determination. A painter cannot "will" a masterpiece onto a canvas. He or she must utilize every ounce of creativity and summon every skillset to make something magical and memorable. Many people never chart the world's best song, write the world's best story, or paint the world's best picture, simply because they refuse to do the work necessary to make it happen.

Let's look at this list again:

Design is: Creative | Unique | Significant | Intentional

Why then must design refer to something artistic? If the criterion for design is to be creative, unique, significant and intentional, can we transcend the aesthetic? Can you design your business in the same manner? If we think solely about our product or service, design is most likely fixed on marketing and visuals. But if we focus on our business *experience*, the creative opens up in fresh, new, and relevant ways.

Can we get creative with the customer/relational experience? Certainly. We can create new and innovative ways of engaging the customer in a manner that is fresh and unique. Why retain the status quo when you can shock the standard system of conduct? I often tell my 18 year old daughter that there is a reachable "bar" in business ethics and attitude. Most young people today don't even acknowledge there is a bar, let alone know how to reach it. Simply recognizing a bar exists already places you ahead of the curve. Design a creative and unique *experience* for your customer, and you can set yourself apart from your competition.

Can you produce something significant in the lives of your customers/clients or employees? Absolutely. You can design principles and practices respecting the energy, time, and temperament of your customers, while creating something new and powerful in their lives.

All this requires intention. Just like the artist, you will not get there without serious forethought, planning, and strategy. Do it well and it flows effortlessly. But it takes well crafted *planning*. In the following pages we will, like an artist, meticulously craft our businesses for greater success. The process begins at the core of your business. It begins by designing *your ethics*.

CHAPTER 4 | **DESIGN STRATEGY 1:**
CRAFTING YOUR COMPANY'S ETHICS

 CUSTOMERS COME BACK, NOT JUST BECAUSE OF YOUR PRODUCT OR SERVICE, BUT BECAUSE OF THE

EXPERIENCE

OF LARGE COMPANIES:

85%	54%	>20%
Mission Statements	Purpose Statements	Purpose Statements

BUT HAVE YOU CONSIDERED YOUR COMPANY'S

ETHICS?

Ethics set parameters, establish non-negotiables, produce success metrics. Determine courses of action & the treatment of customers, vendors, employees and the world.

COMPANY ETHICS >> **CUSTOMER STORIES** >> **RETURN CUSTOMERS & REFERRALS**

LIKE ANCIENT ISRAEL'S 10 COMMANDMENTS

Ethics are not meant to restrict, but to liberate and evoke opportunity.

OUR COMPANY ETHICS INCLUDE:

1. We are not about the job, we are about the referral
2. If a client contacts us about a job, we've lost power
3. Nothing leaves the office if it can be broken apart visually.
4. We are always going to be positive: office, phone & emails

CHAPTER 4

DESIGN STRATEGY 1:
CRAFTING YOUR COMPANY'S ETHICS

A year ago, I met with a man about switching insurance companies. Handing me his business card, I commented on the attractiveness of his company's text-based logo design. Text based logos are hard to perfect. Most look like they were designed in two minutes in Microsoft Word.

Instead of thanking me, he rolled his eyes. For the next five minutes, he recited a story of frustration, misinformation, bad practices, and unprofessionalism. The narrative, and his stalwart determination to not give the design agency having created the logo another dime, was based on the failure of the *experience,* not the work provided. Your business experience often matters more than your business offerings. How do you start to create a positive and memorable experience for your customers?

Craft your company's *ethics*.

Statistically, 85% of large companies have mission statements. A slightly less 54% have vision statements. Far fewer take the time to craft purpose statements. **But have you considered and honed your company's *ethics*?**

No, I am not referring to your personal morality that might bleed over into your business. Ethics are business standards that set parameters, establish non-negotiatables, and produce verifiable success metrics. They determine your courses of action, which reflects on the way you treat your customers, your vendors, your employees, and the world.

Far beyond your product and service, **your ethics *produce stories*. Stories, if positive, *produce repeat customers*.** Science Fiction storywriters build boundaries around their worlds; what can and can't be done in the framework of their universe. In similar manner, ethics help frame the stories others will tell about your business. Think of them as the "Ten Commandments" of your business. In the distant past, an entire nation (Israel) was founded to flourish on ten simple declarations. I believe creating 10 ethical declarations around your business will help you flourish in a similar manner.

Like the original intent of the Ten Commandments, ethics are not meant to restrict. They are designed to liberate and *evoke opportunity*.

Let me break down a few of the ethics that frame our business and recount some of the stories they produce.

1. We are not about the job; we are about the referral.
Most companies focus on the job. They (hopefully) work efficiently, then collect payment and move to the next customer. At my firm, we recognize it is not the specific job that generates the referral. It is realized through way the client *is treated* in the process of completing the work. We put as much (if not more) emphasis on honing the customer relationship as we do on providing our creative skillets.

Clients describe our operation to others with comments such as, "it was such a memorable experience." Having past clients reference the relationship, not just the work, accelerates our reputation among potential clientele.

2. If I client has to contact us to ask about the status of a campaign, we've lost power.
To us, power is the ability to generate effective action. A client checking on a project erodes our ability to act in the future, both financially and relationally. They must disengage from their daily responsibilities to check the status of their project. Power is diminished, and that lack of power must transfer somewhere. Allow that to happen too many times, and you will immediately recognize where the power has lapsed. (Hint, *you* are the one losing power).

We consistently hear that working with us is easy and "painless." Whether they realize it or not, we painstakingly ensure that our clients are always informed on every aspect of their project. We often assess a deadline then add two days (if possible) to that date. For our business, completing a project two days ahead of schedule produces the strongest response.

In conjunction with this ethic, one of our NBA questions is: *"What is the most efficient way and times to contact you during this project?"* By working around the specific routines of our clients, we allow them to flow seamlessly through their day. We only interrupt at times, and in ways, that come off benign and pleasant.

3. Nothing goes out the door that can be broken apart and dissected through the program(s) it was created in.
Having designed for nearly the past three decades, I break apart bad design instantly. A wrong typeface, a simplistic computer effect, or a poorly cut path around an isolated image; they all create subconscious agitation on the right brain side of the mind of the viewer. Poor design rarely resembles a cohesive visual, but a disparate amalgam of parts.

If I can determine how something was created, it doesn't go out our door. Everything must flow effortlessly. It must wash across the mind without a hint of critique, only appreciation and action. I often spend 40% of my time on the initial design and 60% of my time making the last 5% of the design adjustments.

This leads to comments like, "Their work is so beautiful and layered," or, "they make everything visually perfect." Clients create new verbs around our work. For example, clients present us previous agency attempts, then request that we "PFM" (Pure Fusion Media) the project.

4. We are always going to be positive: at the office, on the phone, and through our emails.

Positivity is not just a state of mind; it is a practice. It requires consistency – *despite the circumstances*. How do you test a person claiming to be patient or humble? Place them in situations where patience and humility are not often present. I love shows like Celebrity Apprentice, where candidates defend poor ethical actions with comments like, "I am a person of high character, Mr Trump." Too bad the viewing public sees, not hears, otherwise.

I, and my team, do not always want to be positive, but I do not have a choice. I have chosen an *Inspirational Experience Genre* for my business (more on that later). It is therefore required. We are often told we are an "uplifting" company.

That is calculated.

Nowhere is this more practically realized than in our emails. Once I have completed an email, I reanalyze the message. I want to make sure it is not only positive and encouraging, but I have also added exclamation marks where needed. An exclamation mark over a comma or period makes a positive difference in the mind of the reader.

Whenever any client asks how I am doing, my common retort is, "I am absolutely fabulous." It became part of my brand. One day, I had the worst 24 hours experienced in years. It dampened my spirit. It darkened my mood. Halfway through the day a client called. She asked how I was doing. "I'm doing all right, thanks," I commented, mustering as much enthusiasm as possible. A long moment of silence ensued. "All right?" she inquired, in serious tone, "Okay, what's wrong?"

I felt good that commenting on an "all right" day would evoke that kind of response.

These four ethics serve as examples to inspire you. Based on your specific industry and temperament, yours may be different, but I highly recommend adopting Ethic 1 and 2.

ACTION ITEM:
Take *at least* a week and craft ten ethics for your company. Coordinate with your team so everyone feels part of the development process. Once finished, speak these ethics at various times to your clients and customers. Let them know you have created your ethics, in part, for their benefit. You can frame these ethics in your lobby, conference room or office. Presenting them visually creates an accountability touch point for customers and employees.

CHAPTER 7 | **DESIGN STRATEGY 4:**
THE POWER OF LANGUAGING

THE ANIMAL KINGDOM KNOWS HOW TO COMMUNICATE

Bees through dance   Whales through vocalizations   Beetles through Morse Code

——— WHAT MAKES US DIFFERENT? ———
THE ABILITY TO LANGUAGE

"Communication allows us to interact, but language CREATES THE WORLD we interact in."

 ← Is this a "chair," or did someone LANGUAGE it as so?

BATTLE FOR LANGUAGE RAGES ALL AROUND US

Pro Choice ≠ Pro Life
"Anti Abortion"   "Pro Abortion"

"Control the language and you influence the actions associated with the words."

Design a language around your business in such a manner that you create a new world for your customer to participate in and create action through.

CHAPTER 5

DESIGN STRATEGY #4:
THE POWER OF LANGUAGING

Do you think the ability to *communicate* is unique to humanity? The entire animal kingdom knows how to communicate. Bees communicate through dance. Whales communicate through sounds and vocalizations. Beetles use Morse code. What separates humans from the rest of the animal kingdom is not the ability to communicate; it is the ability to create *language*.

Simply put:
"Communication allows us to interact, but language *creates the world* **we interact in."**

The chair you may be sitting in at this moment is only a "chair" because someone languaged it as a chair. We accepted it universally, because we needed a standard, but it really isn't a "chair." It was simply restrictive to repeatedly refer to it as a wood plank with a back and four posts.

Without much consideration, we accept the language presented to us, unaware that *the battle for language* ensues continuously. Whatever side of the Abortion/Life issue you find yourself on, a battle for language control rages around the event. For example:

One side refers to its supporters and detractors as Pro-Life or Pro Abortion (or even 'Pro Death' among extremes)
Or
The other side refers to its supporters and detractors as Pro Choice and Anti-Abortion (or 'Anti Women' among extremes).

It is doubtful you will hear a prochoice supporter speak about a pro-life advocate and use their term, "pro-life." Nor will you hear a pro-life advocate describe his or her detractor as "pro-choice." Both sides compete to control the language.

In 2014, America discovered North Korea was responsible for cyber attacks on Sony's Hollywood studio. In the media, a battle of language began. The highly conservative *Fox News* described the incident as an, "act of terrorism." The White House Press Secretary branded it with the term, "Cyber Vandalism."

Why the change in language?

Control the language and you influence *the actions* **associated with the words.** It is doubtful the American public would declare war on North Korea over "cyber vandalism." It is a word picture connoting little more than a New York spray paint artist "tagging" a company's wall in digital space. "Terrorism," however, evokes a different response.

Controlling the language around your business is critical and highly influential. Your goal is *not* to manipulate. It is to design language around your company and its products or services, so that your customers only receive the newly languaged insights and understandings through working with you. Consider the following quote from inspirational speaker and "The Mentor to Millions," Keith Froehling. He understands the importance of his brand and shares this description of everything he offers his clients:

"When you live, communicate, and act with certainty, you have power. Create Mastery & Develop Your Rhythm of Success."

"Rhythm of Success." What is that? What does it evoke in your soul? Everyone desires "Rhythm of Success" in their life, business, and family! Right? Of course. We understand that. Keith created a language (a communication style) that is irreproducible. When you decide you want Rhythm of Success in your life, your business and for your family, you must visit Keith's website, attend one of his seminars, or come to him for mentoring! Now, as other speakers and mentors talk of testimonials from past attendees and clients, you're still thinking about how to gain a "Rhythm of Success."

This does not mean you should concoct new words. Do not walk up to people and exclaim:

"I'm a business *stragerist!*"

Remember the words already exist; design them in such a manner that you create *a new world* for your customer to participate in and create action through. Suppose you are a financial planner. What about creating a "Power Strategy" for your customers? Consider the following declaration:

"*Time equals money, and money equals power. Power to do what you want, to be who you want, to help shape the world you want. I want to help you increase power in your life and the world around you, so let's assess your current financial situation and discuss your future **power strategy**.*"

Suppose that as a financial planner you work most with high net worth males in their thirties to early fifties. Are these men looking for power? Certainly! Notice how the conversation was crafted:

"Power *to do* what you want (Id), power *to be* who want (Ego), and power to *shape the world* you want (Super Ego)."

The sentence above hit all bases of Freud's psychoanalytic personality theory, resonating on a visceral level with all of your understood clientele. If you were to discover that your demographic were middle-income mothers, ranging from ages forty to sixty, the conversation would be radically different. But if you were designing your business the RIGHT way, it would be calculated.

ACTION ITEM:
Start dissecting the language of your business. Highlight the standard descriptions of your industry's products and services, and create new languaging around those distinctions that

separate you from your competition. Create phrases that resonate at a deep connective level in the souls of your customers and clients. Test these phrases out on your friends and employees. Then implement the languaging standards across the entire organization. The more cohesive the language inside the company culture, the more it will resonate with your customers.

CHAPTER 8 | **DESIGN STRATEGY 5:**
BRANDING (PERCEPTION EQUALS REPUTATION)

Based on the brand images below...
WHICH COMPANY WOULD YOU CALL FIRST?

LANDSCAPE SERVICES, INC.

OR

CURB APPEAL
LANDSCAPE SERVICES, INC.

WHY?

When we look at a business' website, logo or marketing material, we not only evaluuate their capabilities....

WE MAKE JUDGMENTS ON THEIR
PAST REPUTATION

PEOPLE WORK WITH COMPANIES THEY FEEL THEY CAN TRUST.

Trust often begins at the 👁 Visual Level.

GOOD BRANDING IS AN INVESTMENT
That pays off in substantial dividends in the future.

SPEAK & DESIGN YOUR FUTURE VISION.

QUESTION:
Does your current branding, marketing, and messaging communicate a **positive past reputation?**

CHAPTER 6:

DESIGN STRATEGY #5:
BRANDING (PERCEPTION EQUALS REPUTATION)

    I am not a handyman. I outsource most service projects around my house. There are two criteria I use to determine which service company will garner my business. First, I look for the referral. I seek out other's recommendations, often asking them to describe *the experience* they had with the company.
    If that fails to produce, I scour the Internet and find the company that "looks" the most attractive visually and informative linguistically. I believe any company willing to invest in good design and marketing has the character to provide good service. Am I always correct? Certainly not. But

then *I have a story* about the company that others can learn from.

I do this deliberately. But what most people fail to realize, yet succumb to everyday, is that...

Perception equals reputation.

When we look at a business' website or marketing material, we not only evaluate their capabilities. **We make judgments on their *past reputation*.** The attractiveness or weakness of the design mentally equates to an unsubstantiated reputation of excellence or poor service and shoddy quality.

Creating a positive business history through professional, targeted and attractive design is worth its weight in gold. As designers, we manufacture a historical story for our clients that may or may not exist. Ethically, we won't work with companies that fail to deliver on the promises and visuals we espouse in their branding and marketing.

People work with companies *they feel* they can trust. Trust often begins at *the visual level*. In rebranding the limousine company during the recession, we started by surveying the regional competition. Discovering a disturbing trend, we analyzed limousine companies on a national level. The majority of limousine companies had poorly designed, incredibly user-unfriendly websites. The average limousine rental is around $175 - $350 dollars for three to four hours, depending on the location. The majority of their sites we're cheap looking and unprofessional. I was shocked! Instead of retaining an upper echelon style catering to their demographic, their websites better resembled the mismatched work of a high school student in his or her first digital design class.

In rebranding the limousine company and producing their new site design we created a perception that didn't exist on many other sites. This company was professional. This company was elegant. This company associated with their upper income clientele. It translated into skyrocketing company's sales, during a recession. The bar was so low, that a shock to the system produced an immediate and profitable response.

Whenever anyone asks us to justify our price point, I tell him or her that *we are investment*. Any designer can provide a logo, a product, for their customer. But exceptional companies create branding and marketing that produce substantial dividends. Our rebranded limousine company spent around 1/500th of the return on investment garnered in the first year of the new brand rollout. The next time you consider an agency to be overpriced, consider what you might lose by simply choosing the lowest priced option.

SPEAK (AND DESIGN) THE VISION

In our prequalification sessions we ask our customers to detail their five year vision plan. We create branding and marketing to reflect the five year vision – today. This allows the company to walk into that vision faster. Like a vision board, their entire company image visually reflects their future, allowing employees to see, explain, and live that vision, not in the future, but in the present.

ACTION ITEM

Take a look at your current marketing and ask yourself: "Does our marketing and messaging communicate a positive past reputation?" Do not look at your visuals as information points, but view the design as a whole and ask yourself what story are you telling?

Secondly, ask yourself: "Are we visually addressing our future visions, or do we look like our present situation?" Design your visuals bigger than where you are today. This is not to lie, but to help you achieve your future desires expeditiously.

CHAPTER 7

STORY

I originally left California and journeyed to *Nashville* to write movie scripts. I know what you are thinking. People in both geographic locales thought I was nuts, or, at the very least misguided. Years later, after crafting my agency and developing the visuals and marketing for my myriad of customers, my background in storytelling has been invaluable.

Script guru, and author of *Story*, Robert McKee, is consistently contacted for speaking engagements. The request is not always from University film departments or for keynotes at writer conferences. Instead, he often speaks in front of the top-level executives of some of the largest Fortune 500 conglomerates. The power of story has transcended page and screen, only to land in the lap of business.

Why now?

One word: Access.

Seventy years ago or so, there were a limited amount of stories available. Television was a budding entertainment choice. Movie going was often a luxury. Persnickety publishing houses ensured there were a fixed number of authors. Now, forms of story are everywhere. Print on Demand allows *anyone*, no matter what age, income level or educational degree, the ability to produce the next great novel or non-fiction tome. Four hundred plus channels of Satellite television and millions of Internet programs position themselves for our precious time. Companies that used to ship movies have grown so large they now produce mainstream theatrical and serial releases.

Neurologically, the more we engage in a particular action, the more our bodies desire to repeat that action. It is part of an understanding referred to as, "neuroplasticity." Do something once and you are more neurologically inclined to do it again. It finds its positivity in working out and eating healthy. It finds its danger in sexual addiction. But it presents a powerful insight. We crave more stories because we are inundated with them.

Years ago, you could present the facts of your product or service and retain market share. **Now, you must create stories around your company, your products, and your services.** It doesn't matter if you have a left or right brain temperament; *stories transcend the sides of the brain*. We need them like we need air.

Stories are often employed in the marketing of our business materials, but we fail to recognize that stories generate the revenue necessary for marketing. *I am talking about the power of the referral or the personal recommendation.* On sites like Yelp or Angie's List, and at cocktail parties and networking events, your customers tell stories about your operation. Are you willing to leave those declarations to chance?

So far, we have used the right brain energy of *design* to shift customer perceptions and make intentional headway toward greater business success. Now, we will employ the strategies of the storywriter to further ensure our customers' testimonials are targeted, potent... and profitable.

CHAPTER 11 | STORY STRATEGY 1:
BRANDING: EVERYTHING COMMUNICATES

Your **BRAND** reflects EVERY aspect of your business.

 CORPORATE LITERATURE

 WEBSITE AND SOCIAL MEDIA

 CONDITION OF YOUR OFFICES

 THE WAY YOUR RECEPTIONIST(S) ANSWER THE PHONE

People may forget your company's logo but they rarely forget our **brand stories.**

Walmart

1.8B in advertising in 2013

PERCEPTION:

Cheap • Poor Quality • Disheveled stores • Rude • disinterested Employees

VS.

NORDSTROM

23M in advertising in 2012 & one "Tire Story"

PERCEPTION:

Elegant • Professional • Customer Service Centric • Friendly • Caring

Story Experience is not income specific- it's a conscious and intentional state of mind.

BE INTENTIONAL ABOUT YOUR BRAND STORIES

CHAPTER 8

STORY STRATEGY #1:
BRANDING: EVERYTHING COMMUNICATES

I started the beginning of the *Design* section of this book revealing that business design is far more than artwork. Let me bookend that by explaining that business branding is far more than a company's logo. We will get to visual logo branding in a few chapters, but for now you need to understand that *everything* about your brand *communicates*. A great logo is nothing if the company fails to present a cohesive and committed brand story.

Your brand reflects *every aspect of your operation*. From the literature you present to your customers, to the look of your website or social media pages, to the condition of your offices, to the way the receptionist(s) answers the phone, it all speaks volumes. Whenever my company works with a client on a new branding project we tell them that *everything* is about to change. You must be committed to the energy, professionalism, and story of the new brand. Without it, a logo *is* just artwork.

There is nothing worse than a company that assumes it can slack on its responsibilities because 1. Its logo imagery looks good, or 2. It has established itself as an icon in the marketplace or social sector. Brands go down quickly with that level of arrogance.

A good friend of mine, an author and a speaker, describes a moment where his young daughter needed to find a restroom in an area where gas stations were sparse. Pulling into a *very* well known motel chain's parking lot, he asked the attendant at the front desk if his daughter could use their restroom. The attendant stated that the use of the restroom was prohibited to non-guests. After a brief tete-a-tete with no successful conclusion, he left.

The moment left a hole in his heart, so he wrote letters to the higher ups at the motel chain. He was blown off repeatedly. After months of no resolve, he began to tell his "brand story" (using the actual name of the motel) to the attendees of his seminars and talks. He has concluded that over 1.6 million people have either heard, or indirectly heard, the revenue-crippling story about this particular motel "brand." How's that for (negative) brand awareness?

People often don't remember our company's logo, but they rarely forget our brand stories.

I could not tell you what the Nordstrom logo looks like (it's really just a typeface), but I'll never forget this story. In my late teens, I was working toward a career as a clothing buyer for a high-end department store. In fashion merchandising class, we heard the "brand story" of Nordstrom. The mantra at Nordstrom was that they would take back *any* return, no matter how worn, no matter how damaged. The brand story told of a man walking into the customer service department carrying a set of tires and demanding a refund for his purchase. The catch? *Nordstrom doesn't sell tires.* It never has. It probably never will. But because of their return policy *"ethic,"* the management at the location calculated an estimated price for the tires. The management then returned the man money he never spent at Nordstrom.

If you want to know how many people have been impacted by this brand story, just Google "Nordstrom tire story" and read the comment threads. Nordstrom, through its ethics, created a brand story that has carried well over three decades. It has probably led to countless millions in sales. No design agency can build brand equity for a business like that, despite how spectacular the logo created.

The megalith retail, big box store, Walmart, spent over $1.8 Billion in advertising in 2013. Walk into a local Walmart and ask yourself what "brand story" is being communicated? The stores are often dirty and disheveled. The employees are predominantly uninformative, rude, or nowhere to be found. The customer service department is usually coy and disinterested. Walmart spent $1.8 Billion in 2013 to build a brand story that predominantly fails the second you walk into the store.

I spoke the paragraph above to a group of business executives and I received sighs of frustrations along with rolled eyes. No one in the room considered going to Walmart to be a "positive experience." What was the real brand story of Walmart in their eyes? Low priced, cheaply made items. No care for the customer. No pride in workmanship.

The attitude of *the customers*, not just the employees, reflects that brand story. Act chipper and jovial in a Walmart and be prepared for negative stares and rude comments. Act that way in Nordstrom and the attitude will be returned in kind.

Story Experience is not income specific - it's a conscious and intentional state of mind.
Walmart isn't forced to keep it stores in an inadequate condition, or poorly train its employees. That was not Sam Walton's vision. Nordstrom could easily rest on its brand equity, choosing to come off snooty and elitist. After all, Nordstrom sells nearly $3 thousand dollar Jimmy Choo pumps and thousand dollar Moschino backpacks. Much of their customer base is used to the standoffish treatment received at higher-end boutique establishments. Instead, Nordstrom chooses to *respect* its customer base. It also respects those individuals for whom a trip to Nordstrom is like going to the Superbowl.

We *physically* respond to how a brand story is presented.
Have you ever dressed up before walking into and shopping at Nordstrom? How about before heading to Walmart? There are websites devoted to spotlighting the poor garment choices of Walmart customers. There are none mocking Nordstrom

consumers. We respect the temperament of the Nordstrom brand, while some mock the poor temperament of the Walmart brand.

Have you ever been in a great mood, then dealt with a customer service representative over the phone, only to find him or her combative? Did you return the sentiment? How about the converse? Have you ever been angry over a product or service, contacted customer service and been treated with such respect that you left the conversation in a better mood than you had when you woke up that morning?

It really is not hard to tell a good brand story. **It is simply being intentional. It is a change in *attitude*.** It is not resting on the advertising prowess of a bunch of Chicago ad execs to positively recast what the general public negatively sees everyday after interacting with the company's employees or walking into their establishments.

One tire story from one Nordstrom location from three decades ago, juxtaposed with Walmart's 1.8 Billion spent on international advertising in a single year.

Most of us do not have businesses that large. That may be a good thing. Getting the rudder to turn on a schooner is a lot easier than turning the rudder on a cruise ship. Regardless of your business' size, you can be intentional about every aspect of the brand story.

ACTION ITEM

Dissect every aspect of your business operation and ask, what is my brand position? Consider talking with each employee and see if they can recite a cohesive brand story with customers, friends and other employees. If you find incongruent messaging, consider training and consulting so that your final brand messaging is clear, concise and actionable.

CHAPTER 15 | **STORY STRATEGY 5: CREATING YOUR BRAND'S "VISUAL STORY"**

Great branding equates to visual storytelling

LOGOS: IT'S MORE THAN DIFFERENTIATION

4 major components to a company's visual brand story

VISION
Where is this story going?

CUSTOMERS
Who is most interested in the story?

CULTURE
What are my story characters like?

CAPABILITIES
Who is accomplished through my story?

CHAPTER 9

STORY STRATGY 5: CREATING YOUR BRAND'S "VISUAL STORY:"

One of the most potent storytelling aspects of your company occurs through your *company's logo branding*. *"Wait,"* you might say, "isn't logo branding part of the *Design* section of this book?" This is true for a majority of the logos created in the global marketplace. They are aesthetic icons, fashioned with the name of the company, in (hopefully) an interesting font.

But great branding equates to *visual storytelling*. A well-developed brand *tells the story* of the company. Superb designers are visual – and visceral – storytellers. Instead of words, they use shape, color and tone. Every line and every color block of the brand image is meant to convey and portray some meaning and aspect of the business operation.

IT'S MORE THAN DIFFERENTIATION

Differentiation is a given in branding. The most novice designer or agency recognizes that a developed brand *must* set itself apart from its competition. As designers, if our created brand too closely resembles another brand we risk facing litigation. Even a seven year old can create differentiation and uniqueness in a crayon sketch.

In Chapter 1, I explained that as the barrier to entry in the design world eroded, through highly intuitive and low cost design programs, the market flooded with would-be creatives. Many of their logos still reside on corporate buildings and the sides of fleet vehicles today. While those designers created art, they often neglected to craft stories. They developed "unique" icons that failed to evoke action. At best, their imagery helped delineate one company from another.

A great brand developer addresses 4 major components of the company's story: Its Vision, Culture, Customers and Capabilities.

VISION: *Where is this story going?*
A great brand not only communicates the current state of a company, but also prophetically addresses its future vision. As I said in chapter 10, you must always be innovating. A great brand is not stagnant. It has its own life, its own energy. It is a forward-thinking energy. As I stated previously, one of our NBA questions is, *"where do you see your company in five*

years?" We then create the new brand to reflect their unique five year vision.

This often occurs through the brand mark. But it can also be realized through the company *tagline*. The tagline is a powerful opportunity to linguistically communicate your message in a way that accents the visual or adds to the conversation. A good design agency spends as much time crafting their tagline as they do developing the logo mark itself. Taglines can be **informative**, often detailing the specifics on the operation. They can be **inspirational**, drawing the viewer into an energetic experience with the brand. They can be **questions** to evoke future conversation. Consider the UPS tagline, *"what can Brown do for you?"* It encourages the viewer to answer the question in his or her own frame of business.

CULTURE: *What are my story characters like?*
One of the arenas most missed by brand developers is reflecting the company culture. As a business owner or independent contractor, you not only create an organization – *you create a culture*. People gravitate to various cultural personalities. Growing up in Silicon Valley, the culture of many dot.com startups was whimsical, irreverent and energetic. Would you qualify IBM with the same adjectives? I doubt it.

Based on its brand visual, I would consider IBM to be more of a left brained operation. It draws that type of employee and customer. If that is the customer they are pursuing, they have done their job well. If not, they may have missed the mark for decades. By creating a brand that reflects both your employees and your customers' personalities, you draw in those of like mind. This can be done through color, font type, sharp lines or soft strokes; it all matters.

CUSTOMERS: *Who is most interested in the story?*
A great story brand reflects all aspects of the customer. It must resonate deep in their souls. Story genres often draw certain types of individuals. It is unlikely that a sci-fi horror enthusiast would be drawn to the latest romantic drama. So the movie trailer production team doesn't craft their story pitch to tantalize the person who just caught the latest Alien hack-and-slash picture. Recognize who your audience is (Chapter 5), then craft a visual story that is both recognizable and resonant.

If done correctly, you create brand ambassadors strictly based on the brand itself. Consider the power of the Under Armor Brand. Originally geared for athletes to address the rigors and sweat-laced results of exercise, the brand has taken on a life of its own. It is now worn by anyone inspired by the iconic U and A that formulates the logo. Under Armor became a fashion mark, transcending the company's message and products.

EXPERT LEVEL BRANDING – TRANSCENDENCE
This leads to the expert level of branding: customer (or demographic) transcendence. A great friend of mine, Brian Church, author of *Relationship Momentum*, refers to transcendent customers as *"Unlikely Ambassadors:"* individuals or groups that crave your brand based on the energy and experience of the brand itself:

"It is the sixty-year old millionaire businessman sporting a pair of Chuck Taylor All Stars. It is the 300-pound ex-NFL player who buys a Snuggie and then tweets (twitter) about it."

The best designers create brands that become fashion and cultural icons. When the desired customer wholly embraces the story, the brand pendulum creates such a sway that the *unlikely ambassador* wants in on the movement.

CAPABILIITIES: *What is accomplished through my story?* This is the most obvious arena; which is why I placed it last. Any decent designer will address a company's capabilities in the brand story. Often, that brand simply reflects the most generic motif of that company's capabilities:

A law firm that uses a scale in their logo; A doctor that uses a simplistic rendition of the medical cross; An accountant who uses a rising arrow or a fiscal chart... these are not only basic, they are also benign. They have little or no power. It's like a movie with a plotline so basic and formulaic that people walk out and demand their money back. In the case of your brand, they may avoid offering you money in the first place.

The next chapter will provide you some examples of powerful brand stories, and allow you to assess your own branding.

CHAPTER 10

BRAND STORIES APPLIED

The following pages contain three "brand stories." Before reading the descriptions, try to associate yourself with the potential story you believe the brand is telling. Then read the comments below the brand to see how consistent your thoughts were to the actual explanation.

1ST BRAND STORY: CROSSTOWN

DELIVERY ▸ LOGISTICS ▸ WAREHOUSING

Crosstown Courier was a regional courier company operating in the General Nashville Metro area. Having experienced significant success as a localized courier operation, they were looking to establish themselves as a stronger player among the bigger logistics operations such as UPS and FedEx. They came to us for a rebrand.

What story are we communicating here? First, the obvious; what did we remove? The name "Courier." They are now simply, "Crosstown." This opened up new possibilities, both in the moment and in the future. Secondly, we added their three focuses to their tagline text, using first the broader and more universal term "delivery," rather than "courier." We also chose arrows to separate the services, avoiding traditional dots. Why? To get the viewer's eye to travel down their list of services. Logistics and Warehousing were somewhat recent offerings of the new Crosstown, so the arrows allowed the viewer to engage the full scope of current services.

Then, consider the visual expression. The three services are represented as curving arrows, showing speed, efficiency and power. The arrows expand out to the corners of the circle referencing how their services travel out beyond the local regions. In addition, the blue sphere is a depiction of the globe, showing the breadth of their new operation. The three arrows come together in the center, illustrating the cohesive ethics and vision of the operation.

In addition, the company's founders held very strong Christian beliefs. Their previous logo predominantly focused on the cross, which could often prove divisive. The new design still featured the cross, but it was less prevalent, creating a more universal relationship with their customers. We did not want to hide their convictions, but instead made it an integral component of the brand, rather than its central focus.

2ND BRAND STORY: ALPHA LIMOUSINE

We rebranded Alpha Limousine, as stated previously, during the height of the recession. Even though the company was less than a few years old, the owners had the foresight to recognize the need for a stronger brand presence. After a thorough pre-qualification process, we developed this brand. Based on the design presented above, would you speculate this business might have a 1928 Rolls Royce Phantom in their arsenal of cars? Probably not. But if you were looking to be escorted across town in the newest in the modern luxury vehicles, (such as HUMMER vehicles, AMG Mercedes, or Chrysler 300s) would this be the company to call?

From a sleek modern brand mark, commensurate to a automobile company emblem, to a hyper modern gold fade, to a custom created sci-fi style font for "ALPHA," the brand was designed to evoke a story of modern sleekness and style. We wanted to portray refined, modern luxury. Now, if the company was smart (which they are), they would have a partnership with another charter company utilizing vehicles such as Rolls Royce Phantoms and other classic automobiles. This way every customer call produced some level of revenue, whether direct or indirect.

We also left off a distinguishable tagline. Why? The name creates the necessary association. Alpha is the first letter of the Greek alphabet. It represents power, innovation, and force. It is a bold declaration, on that carries a lot of gravitas. Think of the term, "alpha male" and all it connotes. By calling themselves the "Alpha" of limousine companies, they were boasting of their expertise, their dominance and their bravado. Everything you needed to know about the company was communicated through its name. We are a force not to be reckoned with, *'enough said.'*

3RD BRAND STORY: ARMODA

This is my personal favorite of the three designs presented. It is quite artistic while retaining a strong graphic brand style. Suppose you were in the market for French Colonial Style Bedroom Furniture, do you think this is the right company for you? Not necessarily. But that was not the philosophy of this firm. They were modern, sleek, and cool sixties/seventies-retro design fanatics.

If you were a bar, a restaurant, a hip new business or an individual that recently purchased a modern style home, do you think design this might resonate? Absolutely! The image not only reflected the character and culture of the firm, but also directly represented the artwork and furniture potentially utilized on a client's design project.

While the logo mark was quite graphic, there would be times where the full color logo was not conducive, such placing it on multi color backgrounds. Therefore, the logo name was given just enough customization it could stand alone, without appearing to be a couple lines of standard text. In addition, the culture of the firm was fun and lively, so we chose a more playful and off kilter font for the "interior architectural design" tagline. The colors are shocking, reminiscent of an Andy Warhol color palette. The white pillow in the center of the chair presents the perfect amount of negative space while drawing you directly into the center of the design.

WHAT HAVE WE LEARNED?

These brand stories not only communicate the product, services and cultures of these businesses, they also prequalify the customer. A customer can associate themselves with these companies without any preconception of the operation. It is all visually provided in the brand mark and message content.

Statistically, every business phone call strips away fifteen minutes of productivity, after we hang up the phone. By visually prequalifying your customers, you ensure customer phone inquiries are targeted and the customer is engaged. This keeps productivity high and respects the time and power of future customers and company employees.

Your brand always communicates a story – positive or negative, strong or poor. The clarity of that story is the direct result of the care and creativity of the individual or firm designing your logo or brand.

Adding out of necessity
Failing to create a story with your logo mark, forces you to devote more time and money in developing additional messaging and visual communication. People rave at the Apple Logo. It *is* brilliant. But its brilliance doesn't center solely on the logo itself. It is contained in the brand design and messaging surrounding it. The logo could be used for a restaurant or food product or service company without any modification. The visual messaging surrounding the Apple logo communicates the full story. Yet ask anyone never having seen the logo or having no knowledge of the company to tell its story, and it is highly doubtful they would profess it is the brand of technology company, despite how powerfully that brand developed over nearly the last five decades.

A great brand's auxiliary components *accent and amplify* **the story.** They aren't forced to fill in the messaging gaps of a brand too generic to qualify its customer base or communicate the company culture.

Great branding is a clever balance. Too much story in your logo and it can look convoluted and be difficult to reproduce. Too little story and you must reinvest time and money in additional brand imagery.

Bottom line: you need to work with a reputable and well-established firm to develop your logo brand story. The razor's edge is thin, and many design companies gash themselves on either side of the blade. After the design agency moves on from your project, you, and your company, are left to deal with the aftermath. Spend the extra time, energy and finances to make sure things are done correctly in the beginning. It will pay off in huge dividends in the future. You lose both profits and power through poor logo brand storytelling.

ACTION ITEM

Look at your company's current brand and ask yourself if it tells the right story. Hand your business cards out to others and ask them describe the culture, customer and vision of your operation. Look at the fonts chosen, the colors and the visual mark; are they all on target? Is the logo too generic of a motif? Does the brand need additional messaging and marketing to communicate the full story? If you, and your relationships, fail to answer the questions in an acceptable manner, your customers and prospects may see your company in the same light. Devote the time necessary to finding an effective design and branding agency that can address these issues.

CHAPTER 11

MEANING

"I want to work hard, collect my paycheck, commission check or stipend and go home."

The sentence above reflects the mindset of many American workers. Work is a requirement, a rather extended chore. Real life or, better yet, *the benefits* of real life, occur once I clock out or shut off the light in my corner office and head home. Responsibility and concern are not necessarily right brain energies. But the concept of *meaning* is.

The majority of right brain individuals strive to find meaning and inherent purpose in and through their lives. Remember the history lesson of chapter 2 – the rebellion of the

1960's? It was a generation crying out for greater meaning, greater purpose than the mindset of the sentence starting this chapter. For many, meaning centers on the individual. What is the meaning of life... *for me?* We are often questioning narcissists. We focus on the value of the one, and forget the value of many.

The right brained differ. The great screenwriters, authors, songwriters, artists *want* to communicate something to the world. They see the world as bigger than themselves, or at the very least, that *their ideas* are bigger than themselves. An old Irish quote states something like: "I don't want to write the country's laws, I'll change society through *lyrics*." There is often a higher purpose driving the visual, literary or musical artist. Watch *any* awards show and somewhere in the first fifteen minutes someone will reference how importantly their creative craft influences and benefits humanity.

Despite a left of right brain temperament, your medium for difference making, from at least 9 to 5, five days a week, is *your business*. We don't often view business in that light. We use *the outcome* of business to make a difference in the world. If we are successful or fiscally generous, we might donate financial resources or give our time to charities, NGOs or churches. Instead, **we can create meaning directly through our businesses.**

A social battle rages, especially in conservative circles, over whether a corporation is a "person." Despite the politics of the matter, a corporation has the capacity to change lives, hearts, minds and, I believe, even souls, if its directors, founders and employees recognize that the business can produce meaning in the lives of those interacting with it.

I am confident applying the principles and practicals in this book will produce success in your business. Take them to heart personally and they will improve your relationships. But success means little if you don't contribute something to the world. Jack Johnson lyrically penned this about life:
"...cause it's a lonely little chain, if you don't add to it."

I want you to add to the world. I want you to share your great ideas and ideals with humanity. Regardless of whatever product or service you provide, you have a bigger platform than you realize. That you will soon discover.

You do not *have to* apply these principles and practicals if you choose against it. You do not have to read this upcoming section. Yet remember: there are few people that want to be Justin Beiber or Kim Kardashian. *We just want their stuff.* Can you say the same thing about Bono, Pope Francis, Maya Angelou, Martin Luther King Jr., or Nelson Mandela? They used their "stuff," whether talent, influence, money, character or wisdom, to make a difference.

In the end, do you want people to be jealous of your money? Or do you want them to be jealous of your character, compassion, insights and wisdom? If you would rather be known for the latter, I encourage you to read further. I believe the world will be better for it.

CHAPTER 12

MEANING STRATEGY #1: BUILDING THE "POWER" OF YOUR CUSTOMERS

There are two main ways to be recognized as the most powerful person in a room. The first is to speak in such a lofty and authoritative way that everyone in the room succumbs to your superior intellect and commanding presence. The second is to inspire, challenge and encourage others in the room so they leave the room more powerful than they were before they walked in.

The first way is fairly easy, but it's elusive and laborious. At any time someone else might step up to the plate, challenge our prowess, and put us in our place. More often than not, power plays are a rouse. All the patronizing speech is merely a cover up for our own insecurities.

The second way to be recognized is far more rewarding and intentional. It stems from the recognition that you do have something to say to the world. But your focus is on giving that information away to others, rather than steering the credit toward yourself. Each moment, you have the capacity to build someone else up, exalt yourself, or tear someone else down. The issue becomes who or what takes precedence in your life: your own sense of identity or the value and enrichment of others? There are obviously times to look out for number one, but remember in those moments, you already know what you know, it does you little good to use it to your advantage. At the end of day doing so does little to improve *your* life.

By being intentional and attempting to build others up, you must delve into their conversations and listen more than you speak. That way when the powerful moments present themselves, you are ready to offer whatever you have to share with the world. Each one of us is powerful in our own way. We all have the capacity to share something that will benefit others, even if it is to help others learn from our mistakes.

There is nothing more rewarding then to hear someone say, "You can't believe what someone told me, it changed my life," only to smile and know they failed to realize I was the one that shared the idea. The reward is not rooted in the recognition, but in the fact you were able to change someone's life.

Two ways to be recognized as powerful: the first may offer some egotistical satisfaction, but in the end little is remembered and others leave the room deflated and discouraged (if not slightly disgusted). The second usually gets less fanfare, but you can rest comfortably at the end of the night, knowing that the little difference you made in the lives of others may just change us all.

Working from an Inspirational or Educational Experience Genre requires that you take the focus off of yourself, and transplant it to your customers – both present and potential. Like a date where the other party spends their time engaging in the stories of their potential mate, the ability to build up and encourage your customers can be the difference between a single job opportunity, and the repeat customer and referral.

People should feel good about themselves and about life after engaging with you and your company. This is harder to achieve than you might consider. Many of us default to the negative, and it carries over to our business transactions. <u>Never get a customer to agree with your bad mood</u>. It is a bad ethic, as well as a poor way to retain customers. People may associate, but its outcome is fleeting. **Customers are looking to be *encouraged and inspired*.** It is why we flock to positive films with inspirational messages. Think of your opportunity to increase your customer's power like going to a film: your roll is to improve the lives of your customers during those moments of interaction with you or your employees.

Change peoples' moods, shift their perceptions, increase their wisdom – and watch your customer base grow exponentially, your relationships blossom substantially and your profits expand considerably.

ACTION ITEM

Examine your service and sales processes to determine if you are truly making a positive impact in the lives of your customers. Interview your employees to ascertain who in your organization might be draining your customers' power and mood. Create actionable standards that benefit your customer base and encourage your employees.

CHAPTER 13

MEANING STRATEGY 5: USING YOUR PRODUCT OR SERVICE TO COMMUNICATE HOW YOU VIEW THE WORLD

Perhaps the most advanced form of meaning is learning how to use your business' product or service to communicate **how you view the world**. As business owners, we often temper our beliefs and worldviews in the workplace and marketplace. But as individuals, we are passionate about how see our world and our place in it. Can you mix personal convictions with business? *Should* you mix the two?

I believe it is possible and even necessary. You may be instrumental in the lives of your customers or those that come in contact with your product. But avoid the general misconception. **Do not simply advertise *what* you believe; communicate *the evidence* of your beliefs.**

You do not need to put a cross on your business card, nor a Buddha on your website. That communicates *what* you believe. It often causes polarization, when your beliefs conflict with another person's preconceptions. It also often creates hypocrisy, when your actions don't line up with your particular belief system's standards. Living in the Bible belt, I am fully aware that many people avoid companies displaying crosses or fish on their business cards and commercial vehicles, strictly because those business people's actions often fail to line up with any respectable standard of ethics.

Instead, *communicate the byproducts* of your beliefs or worldview. Most of you have something to contribute to the world, beyond your product or service. I encourage you to broadcast it to the rest of us if it meets the following criteria:

What you communicate should not polarize.
I am not a fan of Fox News. It is not that I always disagree with what is said, I just don't like the way it is presented. Creating polarization may work for commercial ratings, but it's terrible as a business and social ethic. While certain companies create niche market share by siding with one position or another, they are hurting humanity by alienating segments of the human race.

If your message creates polarization or division, I'd avoid placing it on your product box or adding it to your marketing message. That is not to say that *the preconceptions* of your worldview might not cause division. That is something that may not be avoidable. But consider this: *your message* just may turn the tide of opinion on a preconceived idea or belief.

What you communicate should inspire and encourage humanity.

If your worldview holds transformative merit, then it should inspire and encourage humanity. If you hold something in your heart you know could positively change the world, please present it. The book of Proverbs states: *"do you see a man who is skilled in his work, he will serve before kings, he will not serve before obscure men."* I do not believe this statement is simply stating; "be excellent, and you will have a large, influential platform." Proverbs is a book devoted to wisdom and its application. Therefore, I believe that the statement is claiming: "Be excellent, so that you have the opportunity to get audiences with influential people, and, at that moment, present the wisdom you have garnered."

Today, the platforms are available *despite* the skilled work: from blogs to video blogs to ebooks to YouTube and Vimeo movies - anyone, at any time, may just happen to have a "king" check out their online content... and so change the course of an entire nation.

You may even be able to use **product packaging** to communicate how you view the world:

eBars is a company I have worked with for nearly two years. Working with the company and developing a deep friendship with its proprietor, we had an incredible opportunity in the redevelopment of their energy bar label designs. This man has deep convictions in the value and importance of humanity, based on his worldview. When we were working on the redesign of the packaging, I told him he needed to communicate his insights to the world.

What we did was simple and concise; but as powerful and potent as anything I have seen in the marketplace. This is an image of the product packaging of one of their energy bars.

At the bottom of every bar, and on the front of every box, is the phrase: *"Because you are a masterpiece."* This is how he views humanity; and it is inspiring and encouraging. The impact of that single statement can change lives. Imagine a young girl, heavily depressed or even suicidal, walking into a health food store feeling hopeless about life. Looking over the variety of bars, she is hit with a statement that shifts her viewpoint: "I am a masterpiece. I matter. I have worth." Whether she buys the product at that point is inconsequential. He has made a difference in the world with this product packaging.

What you communicate should be subtle
If you are going to employ this strategy (and believe me, you do not have to), you need to make it subtle. It needs to wash over the viewer or listener effortlessly. Don't preach... *reveal*.

Find a clever and subtle way to get your "wisdom" across to your audience. Connect, encourage and respect your audience's sensibilities.

Perhaps the most subtle and powerful example is the door presented here.

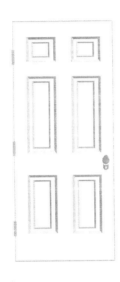

This is the most popular door style in American homes. For most of the populace, the intent of its original designers, crafted over 300 years ago, goes unnoticed. In my home, we have over a dozen of these doors in our home. It is features six total raised panels. But do you see the significance of the panels? Do you recognize the motif? The door features a well pronounced cross, and, the slightly more subtle, open Bible. The original creators designed this door to communicate how they viewed the world.

To this operation, the cross mattered so much that they made it the pattern on their products. They believed that when someone gazed on the door and recognized its significance, it would create transformation. For most people, it is simply a six panel door. But I often wonder how many people have been radically impacted when the intent of the door unveils itself in full view.

Use subtlety and respect if you chose to evoke meaning with your product or service. But if you have been given insights you feel the world needs to hear and it meets the three criteria presented in this chapter, I'd love to see it in the global marketplace.